Wellbeing Workshop

Vision Boards for Beginners

By Shelley Wilson

Published 2014, in Great Britain.

Please visit
http://myresolutionchallenge.blogspot.co.uk
for contact details

ISBN: 978-1514620892

British Cataloguing Publication data:
A catalogue record of this book is available from the British Library

This book is also available as an ebook, for your kindle, ipad, ipod touch, iphone, pc, mac...

*This book is dedicated to Caroline, Sarah and Tracy
who are my die-hard boarders*

Contents

Introduction

When I started my holistic health business, it was the perfect base to help other women understand that their wellbeing, health and happiness was in their hands and no-one else's.

I gave my life an overhaul after I walked away from an emotionally and physically abusive marriage. I had to work on my mind, body and spirit to fix what was damaged. I researched health issues that plagued me to find alternative treatments. I trained in energy healing and other complementary therapies so I could begin to heal myself from within. And I read everything I could get my hands on under the self-help banner. Never did I think that I would be writing for this genre and using my experiences to help others.

Many of the lessons I learned on my journey came from well-known gurus; the 'celebrity' life coaches that had shiny television shows and a million dollar publishing deal. Although their stories were inspirational, I wanted to hear from the women and men who had built up their lives without endorsements and a team of make-up artists behind them. Women and men like you.

I had to turn to networking and support groups to find what I was looking for. What I realised was how powerful our individual stories were, and how helpful they could be to so many others. It was the driving force behind my non-fiction books. My story may or may not resonate with you. That doesn't matter. What I do is pull all the motivational tools I have learned over the years and put them together for your benefit. Whether you are a happily married young mother or a single diva on a mission to release negativity, the important part is finding some inspiration in this guide or from the other books in the series.

Enjoy x

Why Use a Vision Board?

In basic terms, a vision board is a collage of the things you want to have, do or be in your life. It's a visual reminder that anything is possible.

Do you ever get that feeling in your gut that you should be doing something, but you aren't sure what it is? I felt like this, and then I discovered vision boards. The simplicity appealed to me. I have always enjoyed being creative, whether that's writing, drawing, colouring in or arts and crafts. Finding an inspirational tool that could incorporate all of these things to help shape my future was perfect. Years later I would be teaching vision board courses and seeing the effect this simple process had on other people. Some of my students thought they weren't creative and worried that they couldn't create a board. Seeing the look of delight and pride on their faces at the end of the workshop was wonderful.

I started small; pinning a positive saying to the bathroom mirror to boost my confidence, or sticking a picture of Angelina Jolie to the biscuit tin. The more I saw these words and pictures, the more I felt motivated to find my confidence and leave the custard creams alone.

I create a new board every year, normally around the New Year, and then I update this board as the year goes by. It is extremely satisfying to look at last year's board and realise that many of your wishes, plans or places you wanted to visit, were achieved or manifested.

Before I hit the big 4-0, I prepared a board and covered it with photographs of my family and friends. I added pictures of Italy and Spain, and images of fit and healthy people. It made me smile every day when I looked at it. I was reminded of how lucky I was to have such incredibly supportive family and friends. It also represented the places I had wanted to visit before I reached this landmark age. It was like a birthday wish list. If I look back on that board now, it brings back happy memories. I pictured my birthday party when I was surrounded by my family and friends. And I remember with utter fondness the Mediterranean cruise to Italy and Span that I took with my children and parents. I made it happen, and my vision board helped to bring this to fruition.

To answer the question, 'why use a vision board?' I would answer with a simple, 'why not?' I have seen incredible results from using vision boards in my life, and I have witnessed my students and friends manifest the most amazing results in their career, finances and life balance.

I will go into more detail about the art of positivity later in this guide, but for now I want you to remain open-minded and let your positive thoughts create your optimistic present day. Vision boards work as a powerful manifestation tool, and I believe you will be amazed too.

What is a Vision Board?

As I mentioned in the previous chapter, a vision board is a powerful manifestation tool. The purpose of using a board is to activate the Law of Attraction and manifest the changes you want to see in your life.

We all want to change something in our lives, right? I, for one, have made numerous fresh food and fitness boards to compliment a healthy eating regime. In fact, my Weight Watchers leader was so inspired she shared my method with her groups. If you are interested in seeing any of my boards, you can see them on Pinterest under my Wellbeing Workshop Series. You can find it here:

https://www.pinterest.com/singlemum101/
wellbeing-workshop-series/

Manifestation and the Law of Attraction might sound a bit fluffy and overly spiritual but don't panic. In basic terms, a vision board is a noticeboard, large piece of cardboard or a scrapbook covered in powerful images and words. By choosing to use positive pictures, words and affirmations, you will begin to change your outlook and in turn live your best life – no fluffiness necessary.

Vision boards are not a new thing; they were shoved into the limelight by Rhonda Byrne and her book and film, The Secret. However, some people believe that the cave drawings of our ancestors depict the 'coming hunt', if you believe this then vision boards have been around for a lot longer than we realise.

Tools of the Trade

When I run my vision board workshops, I supply all
the equipment my students will need. These tools
are nothing special, and certainly not difficult to
obtain, so you should be able to get your hands on
everything you need quickly.

- Noticeboard or another suitable base
- Large assortment of magazines
- Glue
- Scissors
- Embellishments – use stickers, buttons, bottle
  caps, ticket stubs, etc.

It's as simple as that. There are other types of
boards you can create and I have covered these in
the chapter on Alternative Vision Boards, but for
now we are going to keep it simple.

I purchase my boards from the main
supermarket chains here in the UK. For a decent
sized board (23.5" x 15.5") you can expect to pay
around £3 - £5. For my American readers, you will
be looking for a bulletin board, and after a quick

scout on Walmart's website, I spotted some larger boards for around $13.

It is perfectly fine to use a large piece of cardboard or even a click frame. I use noticeboards because they are sturdy and framed; ready for hanging in place.

Take Five

The first book in the Wellbeing Workshop Series was a beginner's guide to meditation. If you haven't read it yet, then may I suggest you add it to your list of books to read? It is a no-nonsense guide to the benefits of meditating; including how to breathe properly and easy to follow exercises.

I love meditating. It's one of the greatest gifts you can give to yourself. Who doesn't want five minutes to themselves, to sit in silence, have a bath, or be alone with their thoughts?

Before we start creating our vision boards, I always get my students to 'take five'. Grounding yourself in the moment and slowing down your breathing, helps you to be in the moment. And in the moment is where we need to be to manifest our desires.

Don't worry if you don't meditate, or believe you can't. Try the exercise below to set your intention, clear your creative space and get to the manifestation zone:

- Make sure you are sitting comfortably with your back straight and your feet flat on the ground.
- Close your eyes and concentrate on your breathing.
- Picture the breath entering through your nose and travelling down to your lungs.
- Breathe in slowly and deeply and then release the breath slowly and calmly.
- Do this for a few moments, and feel your body start to relax and your shoulders drop to a comfortable position.
- In your mind, repeat the following, 'I am open to possibilities and willing to create'.
- As you continue to breathe slowly and calmly, keep in mind your positive memories, achievements and successes.
- After five minutes, wiggle your fingers and toes and open your eyes.
- You are now ready to begin.

If you don't want to meditate then try this exercise instead. It will help you to focus on the process of what you are doing. Of course, our meditators are also invited to complete this exercise too:

- Take a piece of paper and write a list of why you were drawn to create a vision board. E.g. intrigued, believe in the Law of Attraction, etc.
- Then write a second list of why you want to succeed. E.g. provide for my family, afford a new house/car/dress, etc.

You will be able to use your lists as inspiration for your boards. It is a great exercise to repeat occasionally to check your progress and maintain your motivation in certain areas of your life.

The Art of Manifestation

I have read hundreds of self-help books on a diverse range of topics. The overpowering lesson in the majority of them is a belief in what you can achieve. I've carried that lesson with me for many years, and can still be astounded when I accomplish something I thought was unattainable.

Unfortunately, at the beginning of my period of recovery, I focused too much on the end product rather than my day-to-day dealings. I fell into the trap of, 'when I've completed [insert random task here] I will be happy'. Eventually I understood, and I now have Ralph Waldo Emerson's quote; 'Life is a journey, not a destination' on my wall. This thought process is just as important when we are working with vision boards.

When we are creating our boards, we must have the end goal in mind, this is what we are trying to piece together. Our pictures may show distant shores, new cars and bikini-clad celebrities, but we also have to focus on the process of getting to these distant shores, in our new car, wearing only a bikini!

The key to manifesting anything is to be specific. When I first read *The Secret*, I was hugely sceptical. The author told me this was perfectly normal, and dared me to give it a go – always one to accept a challenge I 'manifested' my first item. I didn't aim for a win on the lottery or a night of passion with Johnny Depp, in fact, when I tell you what I requested you would probably laugh. It was a parking space.

I had an appointment scheduled to see my accountant in a busy village close to where I live, I knew that parking was always an issue, so I thought this was a perfect way to practice. I grounded myself, calmed my breathing and visualised myself driving along the streets toward the car park. I 'saw' my car turning the corner and could visualise the row of spaces. I counted along and chose the third space. I forgot all about it until the day of my appointment. As I drove down the road and turned the corner, I couldn't stop the wide grin that spread across my face, as I spotted the third space was available in the otherwise full car park. I pulled in and laughed hysterically. Successful manifestation had been achieved – I was a believer.

Anyone who has read my book, *How I Changed My Life in a Year*, will know about the blackboard I have in my kitchen. It reads; 'Thoughts become things, pick good ones.' It is a valuable lesson and one we can adopt for our vision boards. Without clear intentions, our dreams are reduced to simple wishes.

I'm sure we could all do with a few extra pounds or dollars in the bank. But how often do we say, 'I want more money' without getting specific. You may as well be saying, 'If only I had more money', or worse, 'I'll never have any money.' By saying this, you are manifesting exactly that – *NO* money. Bob Proctor, author and mentor, sums it up quite nicely:

'Everything that's coming into your life you are attracting into your life, it's attracted by virtue of the images you're *holding in your mind. It's what you're thinking.* Whatever *is going on in your mind you are attracting to you.'*

To create our vision board, we need to get specific about what we want to manifest. If you do want more money, then work it out down to the last penny. One of the earliest boards I created included a cheque. I wrote it out to myself and dated it for when I needed the money. I calculated exactly what

I required – at the time it was enough money to take the children on holiday and buy a new pair of boots.

Specifically it was £485.00. I didn't add on another zero, I didn't round it up to £500, I added it to my board and surrounded the cheque with pictures of tan boots and a caravan by the sea. When I checked on my board several months later, I realised I had manifested what I needed. How? I hear you ask. I got specific and then I focused on making it happen. I sold my junk at car boot sales, old furniture on eBay and received a tax rebate. I hit the total within my allotted time.

It is so important to be detailed in what you want to manifest. Allow me to use Johnny Depp to prove my case. Mr Depp has graced many of my boards, his rugged good looks brighten my day, but deep in my gut I know that I will not be bumping into this man in Tesco. Nor will he get a sudden urge to fly to England and seek me out because of a mystical whim. I live in the real world, and I understand what a fantasy is.

Of course, there is no harm putting him on my board. The reason for this is to help me attract a dark haired man with similar features - sadly the real thing will always be a fantasy. A word of warning though – by using his picture there is every possibility that I could attract a pirate!

You may wish to invite a man or woman (or pirate) into your life and want to use your vision board to assist in this manifestation. You are clear on your theme, specific about your desires and want to make changes to your life to enable this relationship to evolve. Creating this type of board is straight forward.

With such a clear idea, you can set about looking for pictures that mirror the vision you have about a new relationship. You might see a photograph of a celebrity couple whose passion you want to emulate, for example, David and Victoria Beckham. They appear to be a perfect couple with beautiful children and a solid relationship. When you add their picture to your board, you aren't asking to manifest Mr Beckham, but instead you are projecting your desire for a solid, loving relationship.

If you are looking to change career, get promoted or even start your own business, then you will be looking for images and words that resonate with your desired outcome. Want a B&B by the seaside? Pretty coastal hotels are the pictures you will be looking to add to your board. Get specific and find photographs of the town you want to move to. You could even log on to the estate agent's website and find your dream home. One point to remember though, unless you really want to move to the seaside and open a B&B, any pictures you add won't manifest if they are just wishes. I, for one, would love to live in Cornwall, but I will never leave the Midlands because this is where my family are. It's just a fantasy, so I don't add it to my board. I can, however, add a picture of a rented property or holiday let because a weekend break to Cornwall I *can* manifest.

In the next chapter, I am going to go through the step-by-step procedure for creating your vision board. I shall concentrate on producing an 'open' board; this is what you create when you're not sure what you want. You may feel a little bit lost, be suffering from depression or can't quite grasp the vision of how your life should/could be. I love this kind of board. Most of my boards have been 'open'. They allow for our subconscious thoughts to surface and our deepest desires to bubble up. I have manifested a writing career, completed a half marathon and predicted a period of ill health by opting for an open board rather than a themed one.

The beauty of open boards is the scope to have some fun. Choosing images that make you smile, or words/quotes that you don't want to forget is key. If it's a picture of a teddy bear holding a balloon then use it! Be open to whatever calls to you. After I complete an open board, I spend some time in reflection. Everything can suddenly become clear when you peruse your finished creation. In group classes, I get everyone to talk through their boards and share the journey with the rest of the class. I've never had anyone say no; they have all been excited to point out what each image represents to them and their life. It's very empowering to watch a quiet student bursting at the seams with excitement, telling a room full of strangers how negative her job has become and what she plans to do about it.

Whether you decide upon a themed board or an open one, you will enjoy the process, and I have no doubt that you will also love the end results.

Step-By-Step

Now that you understand what a vision board is and why it's a valuable motivational tool, we can start the creative process. Remember to 'take five' and ground yourself, breathing slowly and deeply to get in the zone. You should have in your mind a clear idea of what you want to have in your life, what you may need, or a bucket list of places you want to visit. Perhaps you want to create a board dedicated to a change in career, or to start a family. Or you fancy making an open board. The choice is yours.

Your vision board is unique to you. No two boards are the same. When I run my classes, I am always amazed at the differences in the finished product. Some are covered in images; others have nothing but power words on them. Some students cover every millimetre while others leave gaps to add things at a later date.

Despite the differences in the final creation, they each have three key factors:

- They are emotional – everything on your board should evoke a positive feeling.

- They are visual – whether you use images or words, make your board as aesthetically pleasing to the eye as you can.
- They are activated – we will look at activating your board in the next chapter but for now, make sure your board is placed in a prominent position.

Let's get down to the fun part of creating your board. Collect all the equipment you need (see the chapter on Tools of the Trade if you need a reminder). One tip I share with my students is to choose magazines that you wouldn't normally read. Thinking outside the box can open up a whole host of possibilities and ideas for future development. Obviously, if you are creating a themed board around getting pregnant, for example, you will want to use parenting magazines rather than the Autotrader.

As I mentioned in the previous chapter, I am going to share how to make an open board. No themes, no rules, just pure creativity.

Keep your board handy and begin to flick through the pile of magazines you have collected. At this stage, all you are looking for are images or words that resonate with you. For example, you may see a picture of two women in a café drinking coffee. A picture like this may represent friendship and keeping in contact with certain individuals. I have a tendency to add pictures of colourful fruit; this acts as a reminder to keep following my healthy eating program. You may spot a photograph of a glass of Rioja, reminding you to relax on a Friday evening and take the time to unwind. It could be a cute, fluffy kitten picture that confirms the time is right to introduce a pet into your life.

When you see the pictures you like, rip them out and put them to one side. We are going to collect a pile of images first, before doing anything else. Take your time at this stage, go through as many magazines as you can. You'll know when you have enough, and you can add more, or replace pictures as you go.

If you're itching to get started begin to lay the images on your board but DON'T stick them down yet. Play around with the placement. You might find it easier to group areas of your life together. Have a health corner, a relationship corner, place your work related pictures in the centre.

It can be powerful to use the centre for a fantastic photograph of yourself where you look radiant and happy. A photograph that means a lot to you and fills you with confidence and pride.

Work from side to side, or start at the centre and work outwards, this is the traditional method used in artistic collages. Overlap your images, zigzag the edges and add your embellishments. A concert ticket stub might remind you of a fantastic night but also prompt you to get out more often. A combination of photos, power words and even your own artwork will provide you with a strong board.

When you've played around with the layout, and you are happy, then you can start to glue it all down. Don't be surprised to find that you begin to discard some images. As your creation takes shape, certain pictures don't have the same power as they did originally. This is normal, just put them to one side and move on.

Eventually, you will have a noticeboard that is covered in significant photographs, potent wording and an explosion of colour. Congratulations you've just made a vision board.

Activating Your Vision Board

As we mentioned earlier in this guide, the end goal (vision board) isn't as important as the process to manifest your desire. Now is the time when we get our vision board to work for us.

Before we started the creative process, we talked about the art of manifestation. It is a powerful tool to master, and there have been many success stories passed around to provide evidence that this stuff works. My saved car parking space pales in comparison with the likes of Jim Carrey, who holds one of the most famous manifestation claims that I know about. It was his dream to see the Los Angeles Lights up close and personal. So at the tender age of 25 he wrote himself a cheque for $10 million and dated it for Thanksgiving 1995. He added a note that said, 'for acting services rendered.' By 1995, he had acted in Ace Ventura, Pet Detective, The Mask and Dumb & Dumber, making him a cool £550 million.

Mr Carrey was specific about what he wanted, he wrote an exact amount and put a timescale on it. What he didn't do was sit up on the Hollywood

Hills and wait for his phone to ring. He made things happen and activated his vision.

Unless you have added, 'become a famous Hollywood actor' on your board, we will be looking at the simple methods of activating.

If you've used a noticeboard with a frame, then you will have a thin baton of wood on which you can write affirmations. Here are a few examples of what you can write along the edge of your vision board:

- I am safe.
- I can heal.
- I will like myself better each day.
- I am beautiful.
- I can be a winner.
- I will gain emotional strength every day.

Placing your board where you can see it daily is the most important part of the activation process. Seeing the images, power words and a visual reminder of what you want in your life, will help you to stay focused on the process of manifesting your desires.

If you need some convincing, then try this exercise. Place a favourite photograph of your family on your desk at work. Somewhere prominent by the computer or phone. This one image will act as a daily reminder to pack up on time and go home to your family.

Children learn to spell and read by repetition, this is a similar strategy. By seeing something positive every day, you will begin to think more about your desires and push yourself to provide results. Want to go on a cruise and keep gazing at the beautiful photographs of all the stop-offs you placed on your board? Then work some extra shifts, get up into the loft and sell all the junk you have at a car boot sale. Take an hour out of your day to physically look at your financial situation and see where you can make changes or close policies that you no longer require. There are so many ways for you to concentrate on the results and activate your desires.

If you are interested in Feng Shui, then you may wish to hang your vision board in a specific energy spot in your home. You may also decide to divide your board into the nine section grid of the Feng Shui Bagua (prosperity, fame, relationships, family, health, creativity, knowledge, career path and travel).

Place it where you can see it every day, preferably somewhere positive. Hiding it in the downstairs loo won't do much for your manifestation skills. Your vision board will love being in a busy family environment. My children like to look at my boards as they pass through, and I often get complimentary comments from their friends who show an interest. Kids are natural vision boarders – cut and stick is their domain. Let them join in and make it a family activity. Doing this around the New Year works well for children as it gives them a focus for the year to come. If they have big exams coming up, then a board can work to motivate them to study while finding the balance to enjoy a bit of downtime too.

Don't be ashamed of your board. Be proud of what you have created. Invite any visitors to look at the images and see if they can piece together what you are aiming for. You might just convert them to your new found motivational way of thinking.

Alternative Vision Boards

I want to share with you in this chapter the alternative types of vision board that have helped me over the years.

My boards cover many of the walls in my house. Some of them I take down after a year and replace with a new one, others I keep up because I am still manifesting in that area of my life. When I signed up to run the Stratford Half Marathon a few years ago, I made a mini board that I left at the side of my bed. It was there when I went to sleep and there when I woke up. I had to stay focused and motivated because I hadn't run in any race before, apart from school sports day – which was too long ago to remember! It was a themed board and small enough to fit in my bag so I could take it with me if I were away from home.

If you find that a big noticeboard (or mini one) isn't going to work in your space, then you can create a vision journal as an alternative. You can make this from a big sketch book or a pretty notebook that you have. I've found a vision journal to be effective when moving through an emotional time or a health issue. You can follow your path to a better time or improved health. With the journal, it's possible to write yourself notes to accompany any pictures.

Spend some time thinking about the type of board you want to make, ponder on whether a themed one is the best option or if an open board would be more beneficial.

Another lovely alternative is to create a board as a gift; for a wedding, a big birthday or an imminent birth. Fill the board with uplifting images and personalise it for the event.

I have also used vision boards to help me build the characters and plot for my young adult fiction books. I use fantasy art and photographs of woods, buildings, etc. I have been able to visualise my fictional worlds and see the characters I am writing about. I pitched this idea to Pauline Williams at Writers' Forum Magazine, and she loved it.

Play with different ideas of your own and you may come up with a new alternative vision board that fits perfectly into your life. Feel free to share it with other readers on the Facebook page:

http://www.facebook.com/resolutionchallenge

Conclusion

I hope you enjoyed this pocket guide to vision boarding. As a workshop tutor, I experience the benefits of creating a vision board first hand, but as a single mum to three teens I also understand how life can take over. It is far too easy to leave your wellbeing behind as you look out for everyone else.

This book hopefully gives you a starting point to focus on; it's here to remind you how important it is to take time out of your busy schedule. You are worth it, and you deserve to manifest the best life you can.

Reinforce your learning and tell five people today what you've learned from this book. Share with them the same tools you now possess to create a vision board. Hold parties, groups or visioning coffee mornings and let me know how you get on. Share your boards on my Facebook page – http://www.facebook.com/resolutionchallenge

Most of all – have fun and enjoy your new found creative time.

Happy Boarding

Other Books by This Author

Thank you for purchasing this book, if you loved reading it as much as I loved writing it then, please spread the meditation joy and recommend this guide to a friend. Leaving a review on Amazon helps others to find out the benefits of meditation.

In the meantime you might like to check out some of my other titles:

How I Changed My Life In a Year:
One Woman's Mission To Lose Weight, Get Fit, Beat Her Demons, And Find Happiness
...In Twelve Easy Steps!
(Non-Fiction)

Vision Boards For Beginners
Part of the 'Wellbeing Workshop' series
(Non-Fiction)

Guardians Of The Dead
Book 1 of 'The Guardians' series
(Young-Adult Fiction)

About the Author

Shelley Wilson divides her writing time between motivational non-fiction for adults and the fantasy worlds of her young adult fiction.

Shelley's books combine lifestyle, motivation and self-help with a healthy dose of humour. She works in the Mind, Body, Spirit sector as a practitioner and tutor. Her approach to writing is to provide an uplifting insight into personal development and being the best you can be.

Shelley writes her Young Adult Fiction under 'S.L Wilson' and combines myth, legend and fairy tales with a side order of demonic chaos. You can find all her books on amazon.

She was born in Yorkshire but raised in Solihull, England. Don't be fooled by the smile - she has a dark side and exercises her right to be mischievous on a regular basis. She is an obsessive list maker, social media addict and a huge Game of Thrones fan.

You can connect with Shelley online, via the following websites:-

Blog: http://myresolutionchallenge.blogspot.com

Facebook: http://www.facebook.com/resolutionchallenge

Website: http://shelleywilsonauthor.com

Twitter: http://www.twitter.com/ShelleyWilson72

Acknowledgments

I want to take this opportunity to thank the many people who have helped me put together my Wellbeing Workshop Series. Writing is such a solitary profession, but I am so lucky to have a great team working with me. Thanks to Peter Jones, from Soundhaven.com, for the incredible cover art, and hugs go to Rebecca, my lovely proofreader for this series. Dragging herself away from a holiday to answer my call – you are dedication personified.

My thank you list wouldn't be complete without a mention of my clients and students. I wouldn't be where I am today without your support, love and friendship. Over the years, you have come to my many workshops and listened to me ramble on and on. Not even bad weather or broken limbs have stopped you. I thank you from the bottom of my heart for your loyalty and encouragement.

Last but by no means least I would like to thank my close friends and family. You guys are behind me one hundred percent in everything I do, and I love you all so much.

A final shout out to my three beautiful children, you are my inspiration, my life and my best friends – I love you all to the moon and back.

29224363R00025

Printed in Great Britain
by Amazon